The Great Piano
WOLFGANG AMADEUS MOZART

WARNER BROS. PUBLICATIONS - THE GLOBAL LEADER IN PRINT
USA: 15800 NW 48th Avenue, Miami, FL 33014

WARNER/CHAPPELL MUSIC

CANADA: 40 SHEPPARD AVE. WEST, SUITE 800
TORONTO, ONTARIO, M2N 6K9
SCANDINAVIA: P.O. BOX 533, VENDEVAGEN 85 B
S-182 15, DANDERYD, SWEDEN
AUSTRALIA: P.O. BOX 353
3 TALAVERA ROAD, NORTH RYDE N.S.W. 2113

NUOVA CARISCH

ITALY: VIA CAMPANIA, 12
20098 S. GIULIANO MILANESE (MI)
ZONA INDUSTRIALE SESTO ULTERIANO
SPAIN: MAGALLANES, 25
28015 MADRID
FRANCE: 20, RUE DE LA VILLE-L'EVEQUE, 75008 PARIS

INTERNATIONAL MUSIC PUBLICATIONS LIMITED

ENGLAND: GRIFFIN HOUSE,
161 HAMMERSMITH ROAD, LONDON W6 8BS
GERMANY: MARSTALLSTR. 8, D-80539 MUNCHEN
DENMARK: DANMUSIK, VOGNMAGERGADE 7
DK 1120 KOBENHAVNK

Project Manager: Dale Tucker
Design: Michael Ramsay

© 1997 BELWIN-MILLS PUBLISHING CORP. (ASCAP)
All Rights Administered by WARNER BROS. PUBLICATIONS U.S. INC.
International Copyright Secured   Made in U.S.A.   All Rights Reserved

WOLFGANG AMADEUS MOZART

Born: January 27, 1756 - Salzburg, Austria
Died: December 5, 1791 - Vienna, Austria

Wolfgang Amadeus Mozart was born January 27, 1756 in Salzburg, Austria into a musical family. His father, Leopold Mozart, was a respected composer and violinist. Mozart began playing the harpsichord at a very early age, and later studied the violin. His only surviving sibling, a sister, and he were often taken by their father to perform before royalty all over Europe.

Mozart's first published compositions, which were for harpsichord and viola, appeared in Paris when he was only seven years old. At age nine, Mozart had already composed his first two symphonies. After more traveling, the family returned to Salzburg where Mozart began serious study of theory and counterpoint with his father. During this period he composed several masses and two stage works. In his early teens his father took him on a concert tour of Italy to broaden his influence musically. Mozart's concerts often included improvisations on themes or texts given to him at the concerts. While in Italy he was given extensive musical tests by noted composers, granted a diploma as an elected member of the Accademia Filharmonica in Bologna, and was named a Knight of the Golden Spur by the Pope.

In addition to symphonies, Mozart had a great interest in opera and he continued to compose and direct operas throughout his adult life. In the late 1770's Mozart resumed his duties as Konzertmeister (concertmaster) in Salzburg, and became court organist. In May of 1781 he moved to Vienna and made this his permanent home. Two of his most popular symphonies grew out of this period, No. 35 the *Haffner* and No. 36 the *Linz*. Shortly after his move to Vienna, Mozart married Constanze Weber. His compositional output continued to grow, but despite numerous commissions and concert engagements, his financial needs were not met. Mozart often borrowed money from family and friends, and little was ever repaid.

The music of Haydn had a great influence on Mozart. His set of five string quartets composed in 1785 were dedicated to Haydn, who said Mozart was the greatest composer known to him. Mozart's later years were spent composing symphonies and famous operas such as *Don Giovanni, The Marriage of Figaro* and *The Magic Flute*. He also continued to perform extensively across Europe. His final composition was his *Requiem*, which was left unfinished, and had to be completed by his student.

This genius of all composers died in his Vienna home on December 5, 1791 at the young age of 35, following a struggle with rheumatic fever. Almost immediately there were stories spread about the possibility he was poisoned by his jealous rival composer, Salieri. Those rumors still continue today and have been the source for numerous books, plays and even a movie. Mozart's musical legacy lives on as his works are often found in performances around the world today.

CONTENTS

Sonatinas
   No. 1 in C Major 4
   No. 2 in A Major 11
   No. 3 in D Major 17
   No. 4 in B flat Major 20
   No. 5 in F Major 25
   No. 6 in C Major 29

Minuets
   K. 1 in G Major 36
   K. 2 in F Major 37
   K. 4 in F Major 38
   K. 5 in F Major 39
   K. 355 in D Major 40
   K. 94 in D Major 42

Selected Variations
   Six Variations on an Allegretto, K. 137 43
   Six Variations on an Allegretto, K. 54 48
   Twelve Variations on a Minuet by Fischer 52
   Six Variations on "Mio caro Adone" by Salieri 62
   Nine Variations on "Lison dormait" 66
   Twelve Variations on "Ah, vous dirai-je, Maman" 76
   Twelve Variations on "La Belle Francoise" 82
   Ten Variations on an Air by Gluck 88
   Nine Variations on a Minuet by Duport 98

Courante from Suite K. 399 106
Rondo, K. 485 108
Two Minuets, from Sonata K. 282 114
Presto, from Sonata K. 280 116
Allegro con spirito, from Sonata K. 309 119
Andante Cantabile, from Sonata K. 330 124

Sonata K. 331
   Minuet and Trio 126
   Rondo Alla Turca 128

Allegro from Sonata K. 332 132
Allegro assai, from Sonata K. 457 137
Allegretto Grazioso, from Sonata K. 333 142
Sonata K. 545 148
Sonata K. 576 156
Allegro, from Sonata K. 570 168
Fantasy K. 397 173

SONATINA NO. 1
in C Major

WOLFGANG AMADEUS MOZART

Allegro brillante

MENUETTO
Allegretto

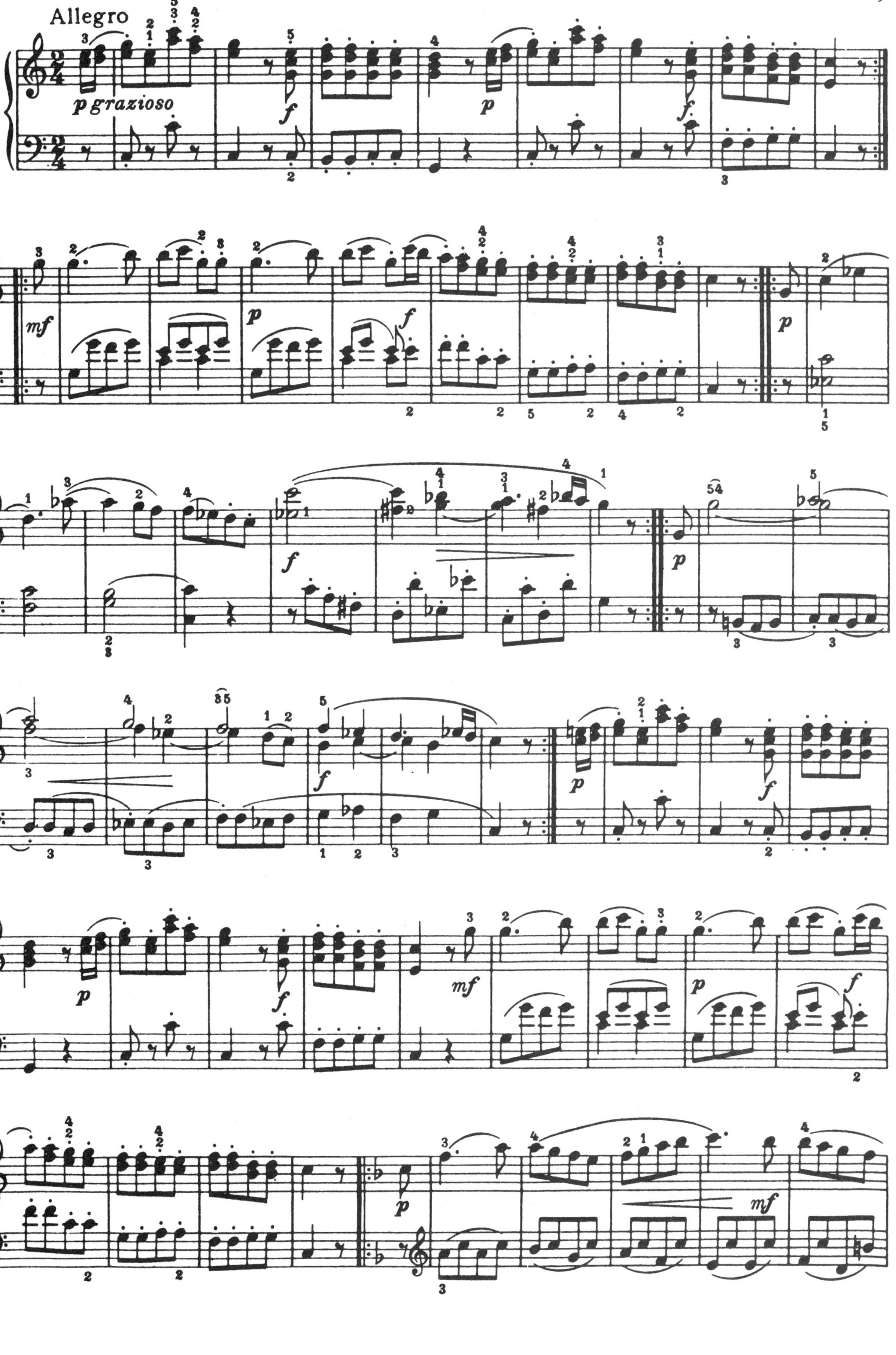
Allegro
p grazioso
mf
p
f

SONATINA NO. 2
in A Major

MENUETTO
Allegretto

Fine

RONDO
Allegro

SONATINA NO. 3
in D Major

18

SONATINA NO. 4
in B Flat Major

22

Menuetto Da Capo

RONDO
Allegro

SONATINA NO. 5
in F Major

Adagio (non troppo)

MENUETTO
Allegretto

Menuetto D.C.

POLONAISE
(Allegro moderato)

SONATINA NO. 6
in C Major

Menuetto da Capo

Adagio

MINUET IN G MAJOR
K.1

MINUET IN F MAJOR
K.2

MINUET IN F MAJOR
K.4

MINUET IN F MAJOR
K.5

MINUET IN D MAJOR
K.355

MINUET IN D MAJOR
K.94

SIX VARIATIONS
on an Allegretto
K 137

SIX VARIATIONS
on an Allegretto
K 54

TEMA
Allegretto

VAR. I.

TWELVE VARIATIONS
on a Minuet by J.C. Fischer
K. 179

SIX VARIATIONS
on "Mio caro Adore" by Salieri
K. 180

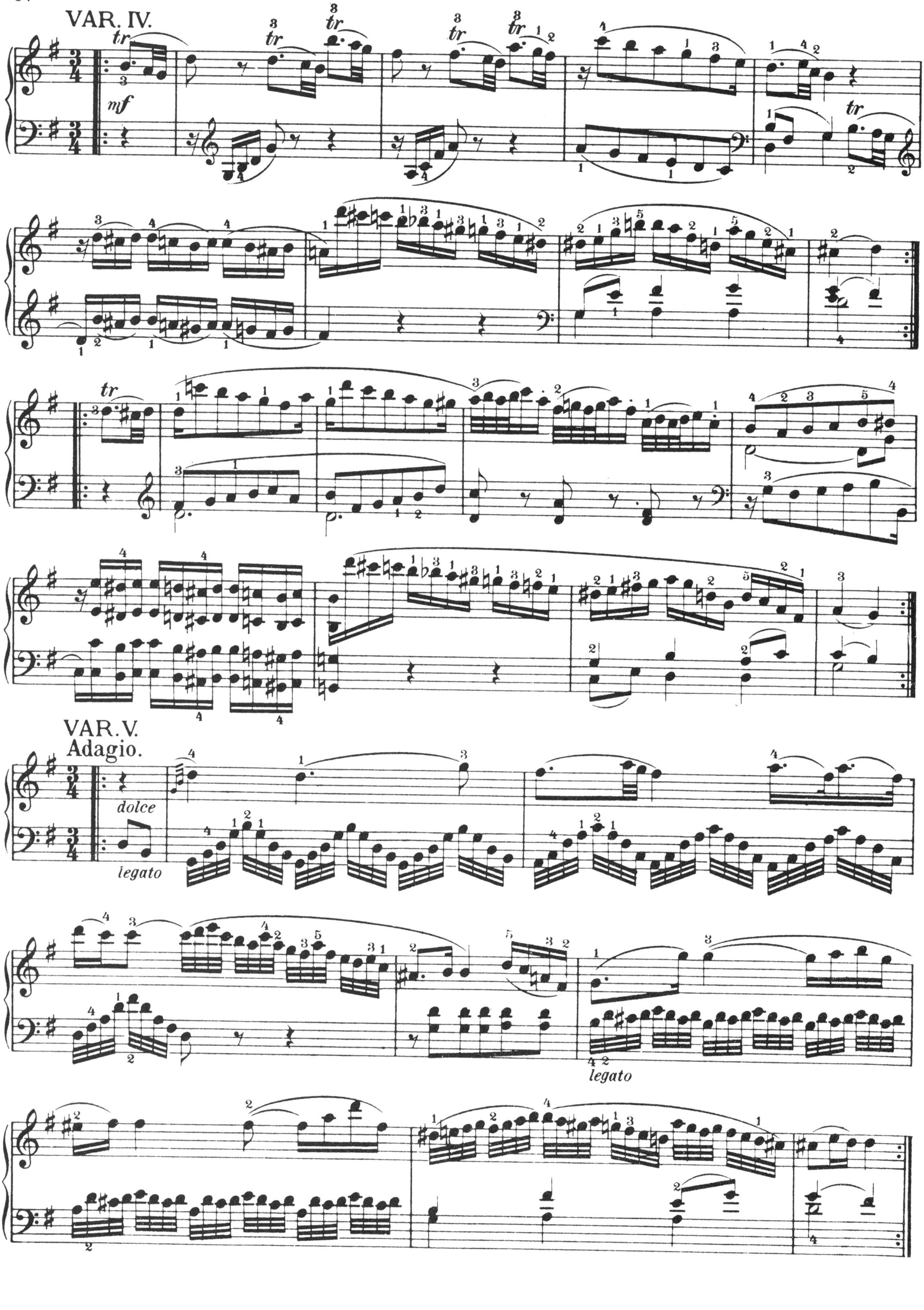
VAR. IV.
mf
VAR. V.
Adagio.
dolce
legato
legato

NINE VARIATIONS
on "Lison dormait"
K. 264

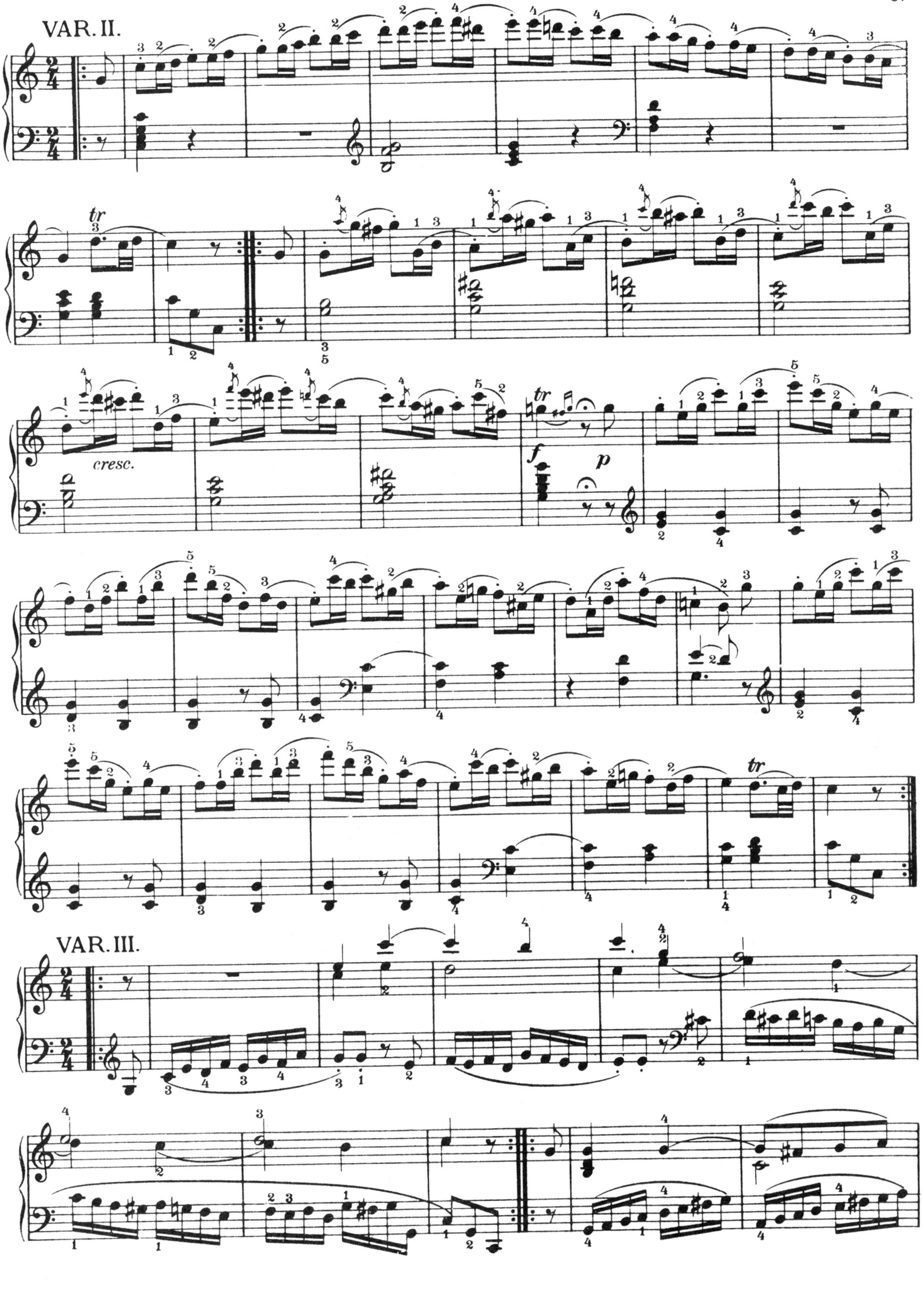
VAR. II.
tr
cresc.
tr
f
p
tr
VAR. III.

74

VAR. IX.
Allegro.

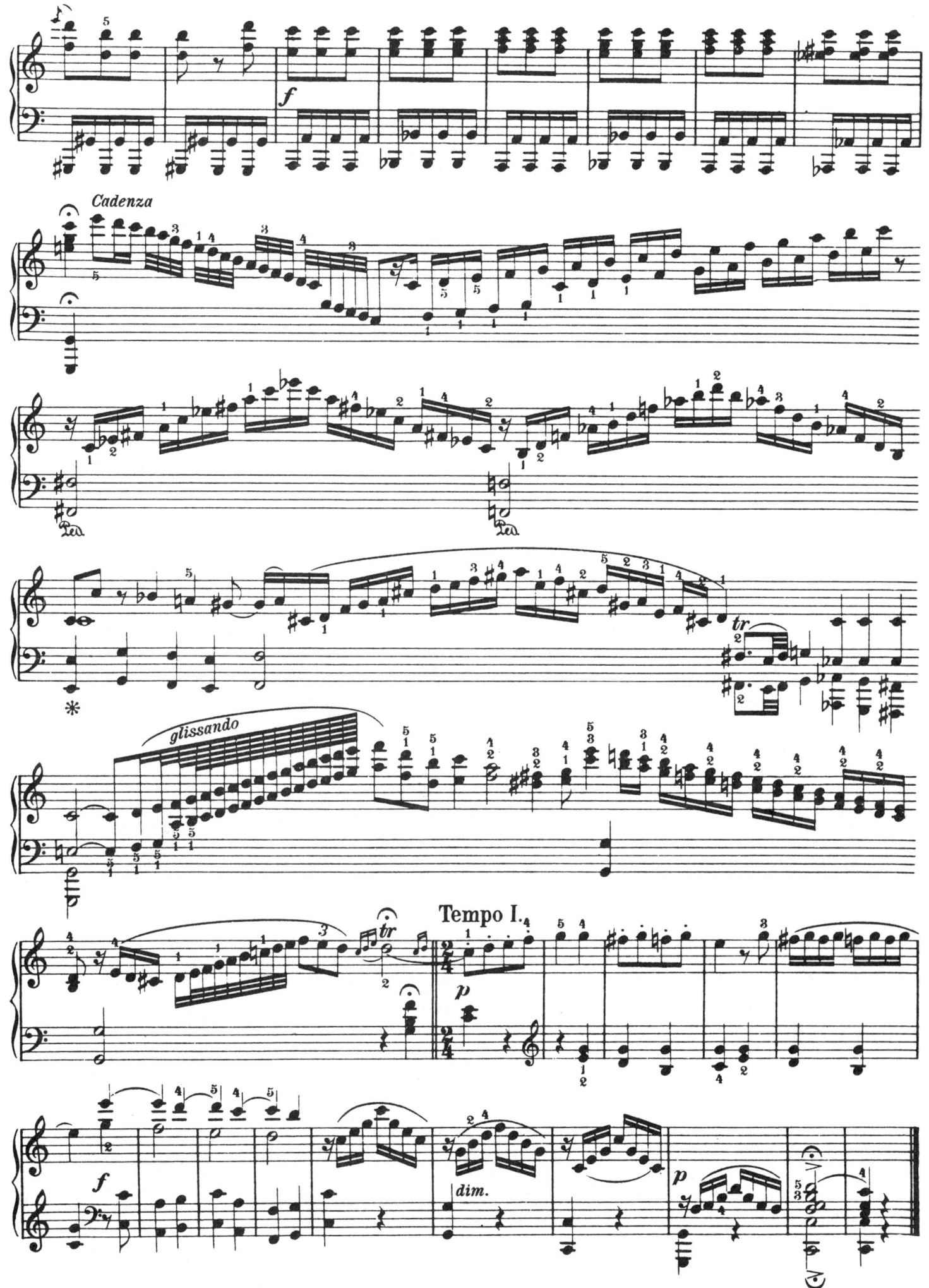

TWELVE VARIATIONS
on "Ah, vous dirai-je, Maman"
K. 265

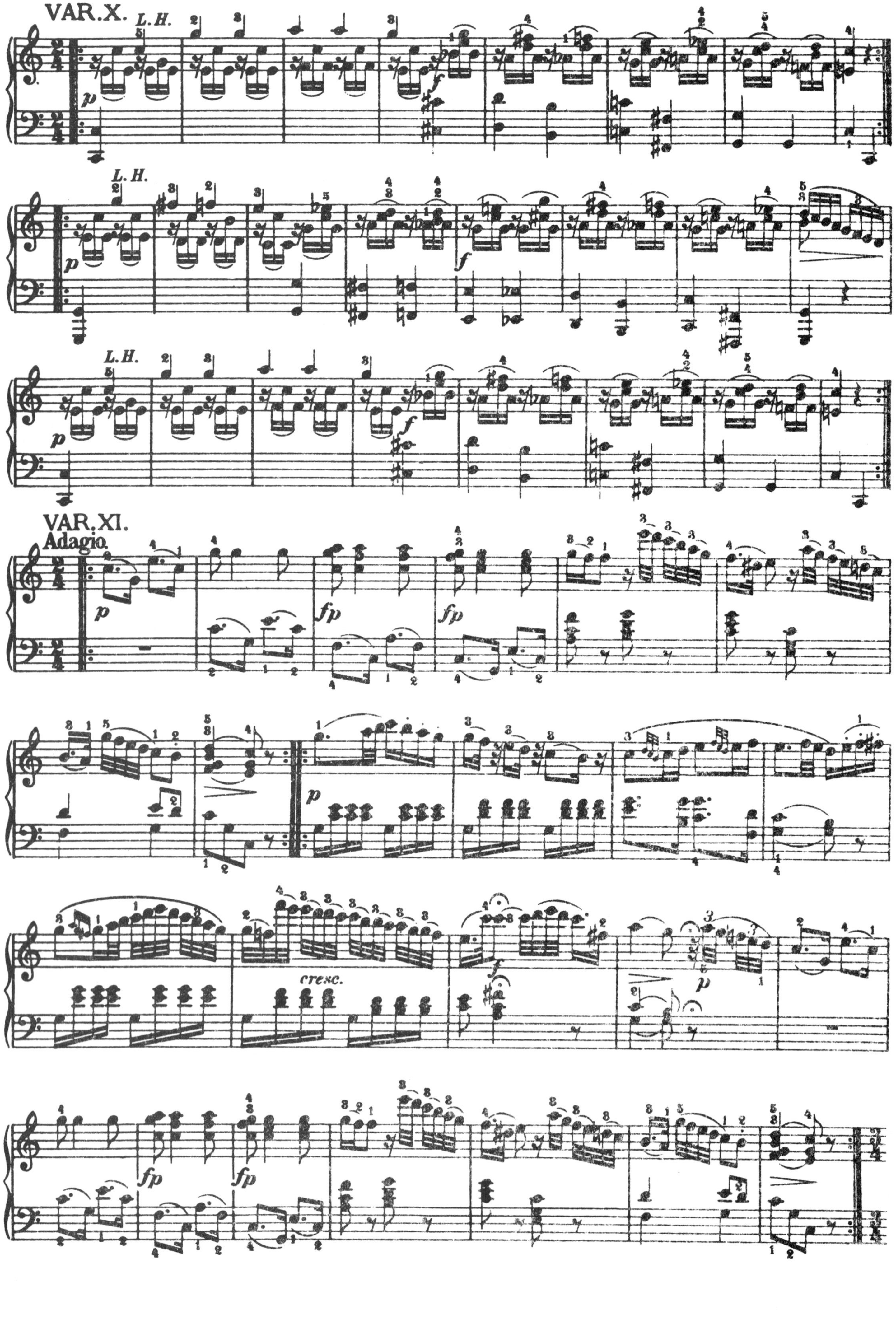
VAR. X.
L.H.
p
f
L.H.
p
f
L.H.
p
f
VAR. XI.
Adagio
p
fp
fp
p
crescendo
f
p
fp
fp

VAR. XII.
Allegro.

TWELVE VARIATIONS
on "La Belle Francoise"
K. 353

TEMA. Andante.

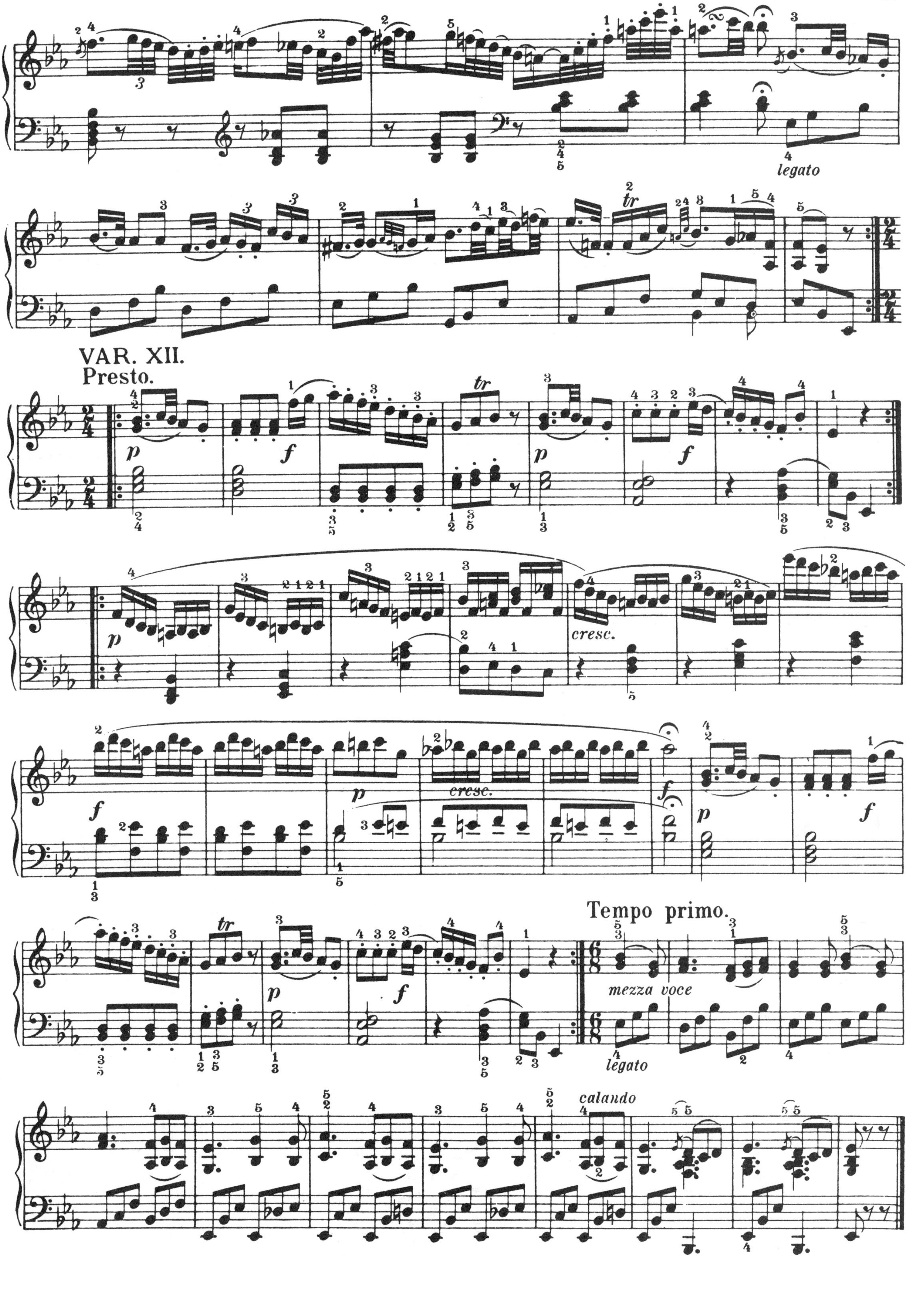
legato
VAR. XII.
Presto.
cresc.
cresc.
Tempo primo.
mezza voce
legato
calando

TEN VARIATIONS
on an Air of Christoph Willibald Gluck
K. 455

90

91

VAR. VI.

VAR. VII.

VAR. X.
Allegro.

NINE VARIATIONS
on a Minuet by Duport
K. 573

VAR. VI.
Minore.

VAR. VII.
Maggiore.

COURANTE
from Suite K. 399

Allegretto

RONDO IN D MAJOR
K.485

Allegro

110

TWO MINUETS
from Sonata K. 282

SONATA K. 280
III

Presto

SONATA K. 309
I

Allegro con spirito

SONATA K. 330
II

Andante cantabile

MINUET AND TRIO
from Sonata K. 331

RONDO ALLA TURCA
from Sonata K. 331

130

SONATA K. 332
I

136

SONATA K. 457
III

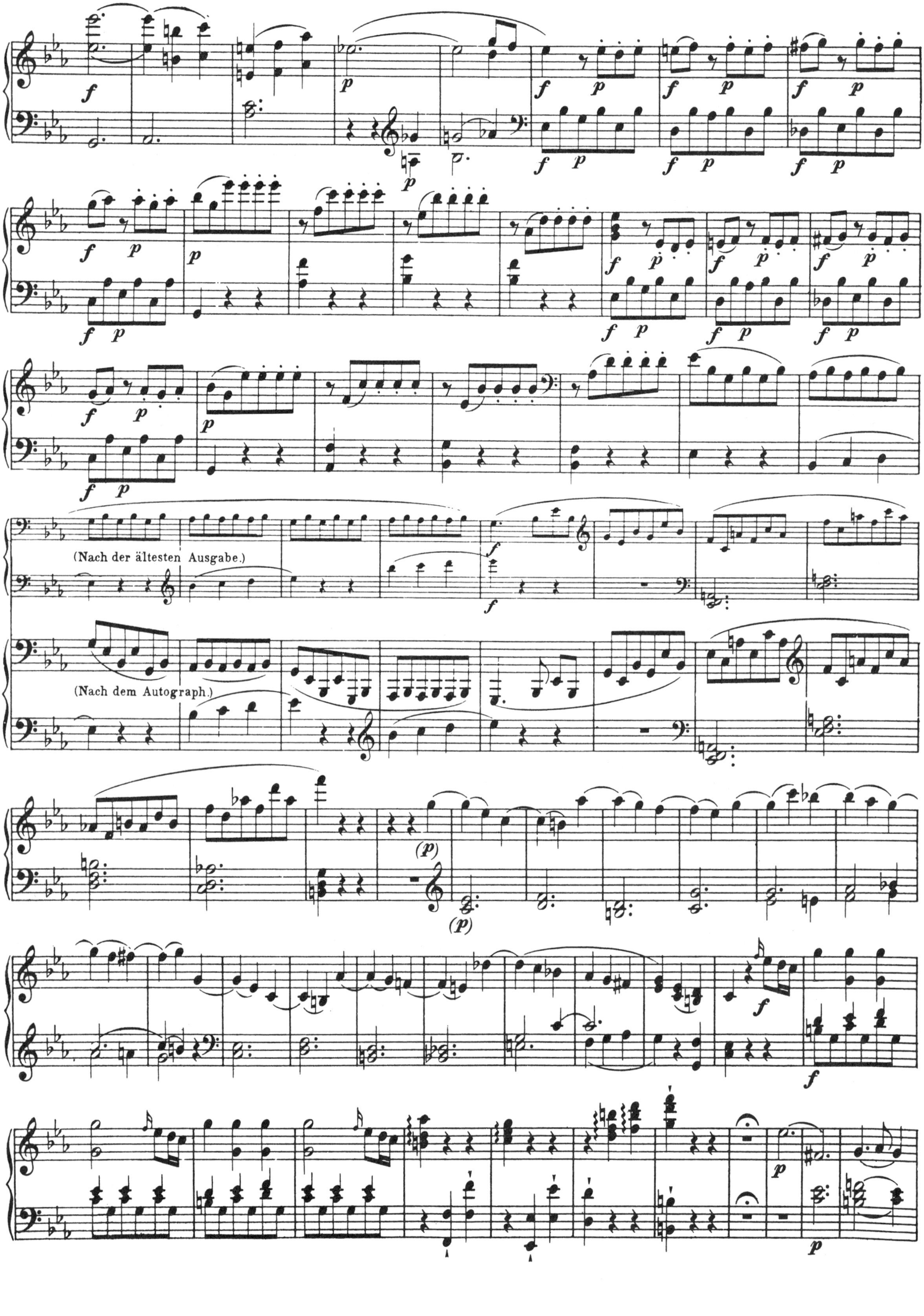
(Nach der ältesten Ausgabe.)
(Nach dem Autograph.)

SONATA K. 333
III

Allegretto grazioso.

147

SONATA
K. 545

Allegro

Rondo

SONATA
K. 576

Allegro

SONATA
K. 570

Allegro

170

FANTASY
K. 397